Food and Festivals

INDIA

Mike Hirst

RAINTREE
STECK-VAUGHN
PUBLISHERS
A Steck-Vaughn Company

Austin, Texas

Food and Festivals

INDIA

Other titles:

The Caribbean • China • France
Mexico • West Africa

Cover photograph: A woman selling vegetables in the city of Calcutta,
in eastern India

Title page: A Hindu wedding ceremony in Bangalore,
in southern India

Contents page: Lamps and incense for a family shrine at the
festival of Divali

Published by Raintree Steck-Vaughn Publishers,
an imprint of Steck-Vaughn Company

Printed in Italy. Bound in the United States.
1 2 3 4 5 6 7 8 9 0 03 02 01 00 99

Library of Congress Cataloging-in-Publication Data
Hirst, Mike.
A flavor of India / Mike Hirst.
    p.   cm.—(Food and festivals)
Includes bibliographical references and index.
Summary: Describes how different kinds of food common in various regions of India are grown and prepared and the part such foods have in the social life of the people. Includes several recipes.
ISBN 0-8172-5551-6
1. Cookery, India—Juvenile literature.
2. Food habits—India—Juvenile literature.
3. India—Social life and customs—Juvenile literature.
[1. Cookery, French. 2. Food habits—India.
3. India—Social life and customs]
I. Title. II. Series.
TX724.5.I4H55 1999
394.1'0954—dc21   98-6976

CONTENTS

India and Its Food

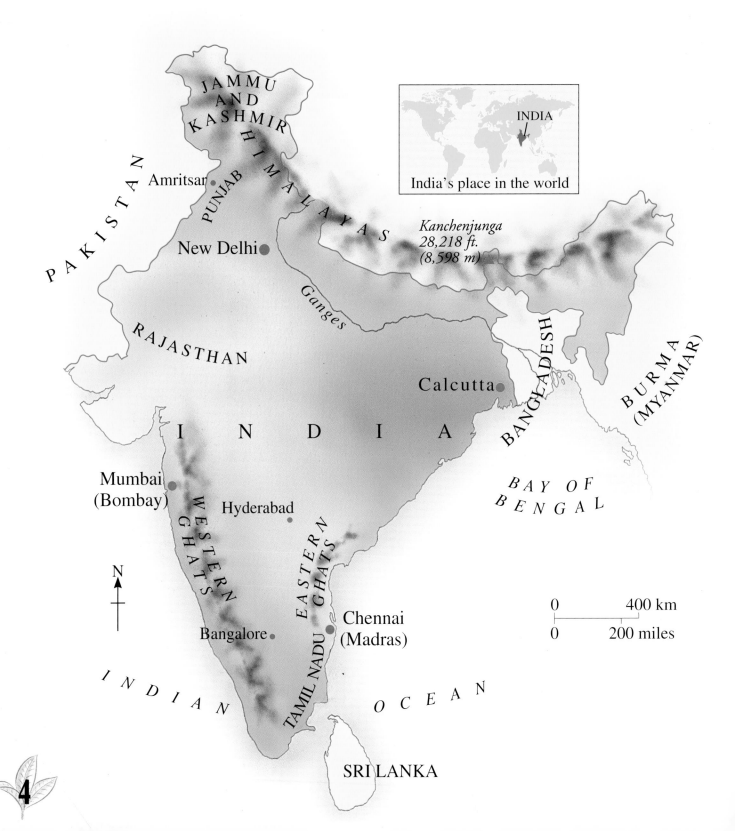

India's place in the world

FRUIT AND VEGETABLES

Vegetables are very important in India since millions of Indians are vegetarians.

RICE

India is the second-largest rice grower in the world. People eat rice with most meals in India, so it is a very important food.

SPICES

Indian food is famous for being spicy. People usually buy spices whole at markets. They crush them at home.

FISH

People who live near the coast in India, or beside rivers or lakes, eat lots of spicy fish dishes.

WHEAT

Most wheat in India is grown in the north. It is used to make many different types of Indian breads.

PEAS, BEANS, AND LENTILS

These seeds, called pulses, are in many Indian dishes. They are very good for you because they contain protein.

Food and Farming

India is a vast country, which stretches from the snowy Himalayan mountains in the far north to the sunny beaches of the Indian Ocean in the south.

India is famous for its many delicious recipes, and food is an important part of the Indian way of life. Even everyday dishes are carefully prepared. For religious festivals and other special occasions, Indian cooks spend days preparing a feast of food.

Harvesting wheat in northern India, in the foothills of the Himalayas

Rice and bread

Two foods are especially important in India: rice and bread. There are many different types of bread, such as *chapatis*, *purees*, or *nan*. Just about everyone eats some rice or bread every day.

Rice needs lots of sunshine and water, so it is grown mainly in southern and eastern India, where there is the most rain. Bread is usually made from wheat. Most wheat is grown in the north of India, where there is not much rain for most of the year.

▲ Spreading out rice grains to dry in the hot sun of Tamil Nadu, southern India

▼ In India, delicious cooked snacks are for sale on almost every street corner.

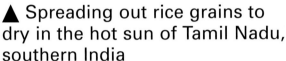

Spices

Spices are important in Indian cooking. They come from a variety of different plants, and they all have strong flavors. Some spices, such as chilies, taste very "hot." If you eat a raw chili, it makes a tingling, "burning" feeling on your tongue.

▼ British people having a picnic in India in 1911, when India was a British colony

WHAT IS A "CURRY"?

"Curry" is a word used in the English language to describe any spicy Indian dish. It was taken from an Indian word by the British, when they ruled India from 1757 to 1947. The British called all spicy dishes "curries." In Great Britain, they used a mixture of dried Indian spices and called it "curry powder."

Most Indians never use curry powder, or the word "curry." They always use a different mixture of fresh spices in each dish they cook.

▲ Spices add color as well as flavor to Indian foods.

SPICE FACTS

• Ginger comes from the stem of a ginger plant.

• Chilies are the pods of a capsicum bush.

• Turmeric powder is made by grinding the roots of the turmeric plant.

The most common spices used in India are turmeric, ginger, garlic, coriander seeds, or cloves. Most Indian spices need a hot climate, so many are grown in the southwest. However, one spice, called saffron, comes from Kashmir in the far north. Saffron comes from the crocus flower. Indian cooks use it to give rice a delicate flavor.

Peas, Beans, and Lentils

Different kinds of beans for sale in Rajasthan, northwest India

Other important foods in India are pulses such as peas, beans, and lentils. There are several types of beans grown in India, such as red kidney beans, chickpeas, *moon dal*, and *masoor dal*. They are all used to cook a kind of stew, called *dal*. Pulses contain a lot of protein, which helps the body grow and stay fit, so *dal* is very healthy. Flavored with spices, *dal* is also delicious.

Regional Food

Each region of India has its own special dishes. People in Kashmir eat a kind of *nan* bread, stuffed with fruit and nuts, called *Kashmiri nan*. Near the coast, people eat lots of fish and seafood. In the port of Mumbai (Bombay), you might eat a dish called "Bombay duck"—not a duck at all, but a small fish that local fishermen catch. In southern India, people like to eat soft, boiled rice cakes called *idlis* and crispy pancakes called *dosas*.

Fish from the Bay of Bengal, off India's eastern coast. Spicy fish dishes are popular in places near the ocean and rivers or lakes.

A Hindu Wedding

About four out of every five Indians is a Hindu. They follow the religious teachings of Hinduism and worship the Hindu gods.

Marriage is one of the most important events in a Hindu's life. When a Hindu couple get married, all their friends and family gather to celebrate. In the countryside, the whole village often comes to the wedding.

Guests at a wedding feast in the countryside, eating from palm leaves

Feast!

Wherever the wedding takes place, it is always followed by a huge feast, with enough food for hundreds or even thousands of people. The party, with singing, dancing, and eating, can last as long as three days!

Many Hindus are vegetarians, which means they do not eat meat. At a Hindu wedding feast, there may not be any meat dishes at all. But there is sure to be a huge choice of spicy vegetable dishes.

▲ Cows are specially sacred animals to Hindus, so Hindus never eat beef.

◀ Food for a feast, including rice, poppadums, and a selection of curries.

Vegetable dishes are named after the Hindi words for the vegetables they contain. *Gobi masaledar* means "spicy cauliflower" in Hindi. *Gobi* means "cauliflower" and *masaledar* means "spicy." There's a recipe for *gobi masaledar* on page 15.

To go with your vegetables at a wedding, you would also eat rice and breads, *dal*, pickles, and tasty side dishes called chutneys.

Spicy cauliflower and potatoes

Gobi Masaledar

INGREDIENTS

1 large cauliflower, broken into small pieces
1 onion, 4 cloves garlic and 2-in. (5 cm) ginger, peeled and chopped
8 Tablespoons vegetable oil
1/2 teaspoon turmeric
1 large tomato, chopped
Fresh coriander leaves, chopped

1 small green chili, chopped
2 teaspoons ground coriander
1 teaspoon ground cumin
1 teaspoon garam masala (a mixture of ground chili, cumin, and coriander)
2 teaspoons salt
Juice of 1/2 a small lemon

1 Put the garlic, ginger, and onion into the processor with 4 tablespoons of water. Blend into a paste.

2 Ask an adult to heat the oil gently in the saucepan and pour in the paste. Add the turmeric and fry for about 5 minutes.

3 Add the chopped tomato, coriander leaves, and chili and fry for another 2 minutes.

4 Add all the other ingredients and 1/4 cup (100 ml) water. Cook on a low heat for 30–40 minutes, stirring every 10 minutes.

Always be careful with frying. Ask an adult to help you.

The Wedding Ceremony

For the wedding ceremony, the bride wears a bright-red *sari* with gold thread. Her hands are decorated with patterns of henna dye. She sits under a canopy, opposite the bridegroom and in front of a sacred fire. A priest puts a cord around the couple's shoulders to join them together. Then the bride and bridegroom walk around the fire seven times, to show that they will go through the rest of their lives together.

▼ Painting traditional patterns on the bride's hands using henna

A wedding ceremony ▶ in the city of Bangalore

CONFETTI

At the end of the wedding ceremony, guests throw rose petals and rice over the couple for good luck. Rice is a symbol for a new life and shows that everyone hopes the couple will have children. The tradition of throwing confetti at a wedding comes from this custom.

Ramadan and Id-ul-Fitr

As well as the Hindu religion, India has a very large Muslim community. There are about 100 million Muslims in India.

Ramadan is an important religious festival for India's Muslims. It is a time of fasting, which lasts for a month. During Ramadan, Muslims do not eat or drink anything during the hours of daylight. This is written in the Muslim holy book, the Koran. It reminds Muslims that all their food comes from their god, Allah.

Before entering a mosque to pray, Muslims take off their shoes and wash to show their respect.

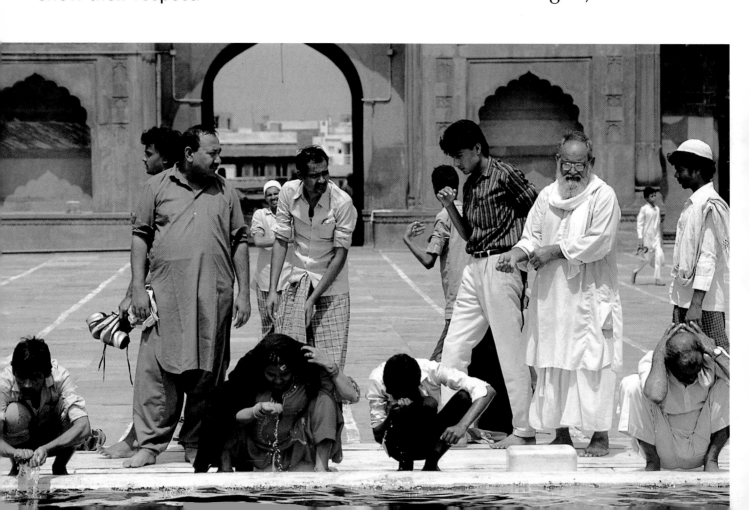

Breaking the Fast

Each evening when the sun sets, Muslim families get together for a meal. They are thankful that they have kept the fast for another day.

At the end of Ramadan, Muslims celebrate the holiday of Id-ul-Fitr. They exchange presents and visit friends and relations. Since the fasting is over, they also enjoy a special Id-ul-Fitr meal.

HALAL MEAT

Muslims should only eat meat where the animal has been killed in a special way, which is set out in the Muslim law books. Meat prepared in this way is called "halal."

The men of a Muslim family break the day's fast during Ramadan.

Id-ul-Fitr

The Id-ul-Fitr meal often begins with a light dish of sweet dates. For the main course, there is usually some meat. Muslims never eat pork or bacon because they believe that meat from pigs is unclean. However, many Muslims like to eat chicken or lamb, and kebabs are a Muslim specialty.

One of the most famous Muslim recipes, from northern India, is tandoori chicken. The chicken is smeared with a spicy red paste and then baked in a clay oven, called a *tandoor*.

RAITA

Raita is a simple side dish made with yogurt. It is delicious eaten with spicy kebabs or tandoori chicken. If the hot spices are burning your tongue, a mouthful of raita cools it down again. *Raita* is always best to eat when it is chilled. There is a recipe for *raita* on page 21.

Making treats ▶ for Id-ul-Fitr

Raita

EQUIPMENT

Colander   Chopping board
Vegetable peeler Knife
Saucepan   Grater

INGREDIENTS

2 cups (500 g) yogurt
2 medium-sized potatoes
$1/2$ cucumber
1 teaspoon caraway seeds
1 teaspoon garam masala (a mixture
  of ground chili, cumin, and coriander)
Pinch of salt

1 Peel the potatoes and chop them into cubes.

2 Boil them in a saucepan of water for about 10 minutes, until they are just soft. Ask an adult to drain them and leave them to cool.

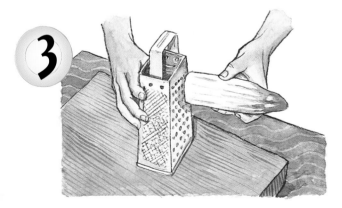

3 Peel the cucumber, then grate it, using the larger holes in the grater.

4 Mix the potatoes, cucumber, and other ingredients into the yogurt. Put the mixture in the refrigerator for a couple of hours before serving.

Always be careful with knives. Ask an adult to help you.

Guru Nanak's Birthday

The Sikh religion comes from the northern parts of India and Pakistan. The first Sikh teacher was Guru Nanak, who was born in 1469. He was friendly to both Muslims and Hindus. In his teachings, Guru Nanak tried to join ideas from both the Muslim and Hindu religions.

▲ This painting shows Guru Nanak, with two sons and two followers.

A Sikh woman ▶ reading from the *Guru Granth Sahib*, the Sikh holy book

Today there are Sikh communities in northern India, in all of India's big cities, and in many other places around the world.

Reading at the Temple

Every November, Sikhs celebrate Guru Nanak's birthday. Each community gathers at its local temple, called a *gurdwara*. For the two days and nights leading up to the guru's birthday, men and women from the community take turns reading the Sikh holy book, the *Guru Granth Sahib*.

Everyone who hears the book being read eats a small portion of a confection called *karah parshad*. *Parshad* means "blessing."

▲ Sikh men wear turbans as a sign of their religion.

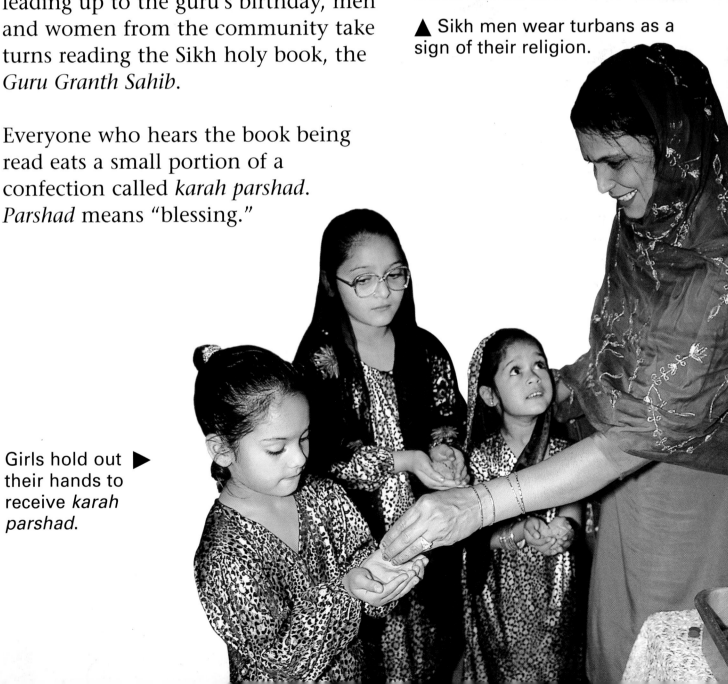

Girls hold out ▶ their hands to receive *karah parshad*.

Cooking in the Temple

▼ Sikhs eating in the Golden Temple, in Amritsar

Every Sikh temple has its own kitchen, called a *langar*. This is where the *karah parshad* is prepared.

Sikhs believe that no member of the community should ever be allowed to go hungry. So besides *parshad*, the cooks in the *langar* prepare other food for people who come to the temple. This is usually bread, *dal*, and vegetables.

At the most famous of all Sikh temples, the Golden Temple in Amritsar, many thousands of people are fed on Guru Nanak's birthday. Several servings are needed for everyone to eat.

BARFI

Barfi is a sweet confection. Like *karah parshad*, it is used by both Sikhs and Hindus as a blessing. Worshipers often receive small pieces of *barfi* when they visit a temple. There is a recipe for *barfi* on page 25.

Barfi

EQUIPMENT

Shallow dish or pan, lined with waxed paper
Knife
Deep saucepan

INGREDIENTS

$1^3/_4$ cups (125 g) dry milk powder

$1^1/_4$ cups (250 g) granulated sugar

5 Cardamom pods, crushed

12 Pistachio nuts, shelled and chopped

Butter or margarine

Put the sugar and $^1/_4$ cup (125 ml) water in a deep saucepan. Boil the water and then allow to simmer for 6 to 7 minutes, until the mixture turns into a syrup.

Crush the cardamom pods and remove the seeds. Add seeds to saucepan along with powdered milk. Mix well.

Rub butter over the waxed paper in the dish and pour in the mixture. Leave to cool.

When the *barfi* has set, cut it into squares or diamond-shaped pieces.

Always be careful with hot liquid. Ask an adult to help you.

Divali

Around the same time as Guru Nanak's Birthday, Hindus celebrate Divali, the Festival of Light.

At Divali, Hindus celebrate the story of one of their most popular gods, King Rama. Rama was born as a wealthy prince, but was forced to leave home by his wicked relatives. For many years he lived in the forest. Then his beautiful wife, Sita, was kidnaped by a demon called Ravana.

▼ This actor is playing the part of Hanuman, the monkey god, in a play of the Rama story.

This Divali poster ▶ shows Sarasvati, the goddess of knowledge (left), Lakshmi, the goddess of wealth (center), and Ganesh, the elephant god who brings good luck.

Lamps and Candles

Rama bravely set out to rescue Sita. Helped by Hanuman, the monkey god, Rama finally killed the demon and returned to his home city. There the people made him king.

At Divali, Hindus celebrate Rama's return home. They light tiny oil lamps and candles to show him the way home. Temples are ablaze with flickering lamps, and people light up their doorways, windows, and balconies.

Lamps and incense for Divali

Sweets and Snacks at Divali

▼ Cooking *jalebis*, a sweet snack, in Rajasthan

Divali is a time for parties and to visit friends and relatives. It is a tradition to take a gift of sweets to anyone you visit.

There are many kinds of rich, sticky sweet snacks to choose from. *Jalebis* are swirls of sugary batter, fried in oil. *Gulab jamuns* are sweet dumplings in a gooey syrup.

STREET FOOD

At Divali, roadsides in India are packed with food stands. They sell sweet snacks, savory snacks, or milky drinks. *Lassi* is a popular drink made out of yogurt, flavored with sugar, salt, or different fruits. There's a recipe for banana *lassi* on page 29.

Banana *Lassi*

INGREDIENTS

2 cups (500g) yogurt
1 cup (250 ml) ice water
4 ripe bananas
2 tablespoons sugar

EQUIPMENT

Measuring cup   Food processor
Knife   or blender

1 Measure out exactly 1 cup (250 ml) of ice water.

2 Peel and slice the bananas.

3 Put the yogurt, water, bananas, and sugar (if you want it) in a food processor and mix until everything is a smooth, thick liquid.

4 Serve in tall glasses.

Be careful with the knife and food processor. Ask an adult to help you.

Glossary

Chapatis Round, flat Indian breads. *Chapatis* are flat because they are made without yeast, so they do not rise when they are cooked.

Chutney A mixture of fruits or vegetables, spices and sugar, that is served as a side dish.

Fasting Giving up eating and drinking.

Henna dye Brown powder from the henna plant, which is made into a paste and used to decorate a bride's hands and feet.

Hinduism The main religion practiced in India. Hindus believe there is one God, but that God has many forms. A Hindu chooses one or more of these forms to worship.

Kebabs Small pieces of meat or vegetable cooked on a skewer.

Muslim A follower of Islam. Muslims believe in one God, Allah, and try to live their lives by doing exactly what Allah wants them to do.

Nan A type of bread that has a little yeast added to it to make it rise slightly.

Pulses Edible seeds, such as lentils, peas, and many kinds of beans, such as kidney beans and black beans.

Purees Small, puffy breads, which are deep-fried in a pan of hot oil.

Sari A long piece of cloth, wrapped around the body and over one shoulder, which is the traditional dress of Indian women.

Sikhism An Indian religion, which was begun in the sixteenth century by Guru Nanak.

Vegetarians People who choose not to eat meat.

Books to Read

Cumming, David. *India* (Country Insights). Austin, TX: Raintree Steck-Vaughn, 1997.

Denny, Roz. *A Taste of India* (Food Around the World). Austin, TX: Thomson Learning, 1994.

Kagaa, Falaq. *India* (Festivals of the World). Milwaukee, WI: Gareth Stevens, Inc., 1997.

Kaur, Sharon. *Food in India* (International Food History). Vero Beach, FL: Rourke Publishing, 1989.

Kerven, Rosalind. *Id-ul-Fitr* (A World of Holidays). Austin, TX: Raintree Steck-Vaughn, 1997.

Photograph and artwork acknowledgments
The publishers would like to thank the following for contributing to the pictures in this book:
Cephas 16; Chapel Studios 19, 20 (top), 22 (bottom), 24 (main), 26 (right); David Cumming 13 (top); Eye Ubiquitous *Title page*, 7 (top), 9, 10, 11, 12, 23 (top); Impact *Cover photo*; Pankaj Shah 6; Bruce Coleman 7 (bottom); Getty Images 8, 13 (bottom), 28; Christine Osborne 23 (bottom); Peter Sanders 14, 18, 20 (bottom), 24 (inset); TRIP 26 (left); Wayland Picture Library *Contents page*, 22 (top), 27.
Fruit and vegetable artwork is by Tina Barber. Map artwork on page 4 is by Hardlines.
Step-by-step recipe artwork is by Judy Stevens.

Index

Page numbers in **bold** mean there is a photograph on the page.